Families Are Forever

Strengthening Bonds in Times of Challenge

By

Sarah Tancredi

TABLE OF CONTENTS

INTRODUCTION

CHAPTER 1
Defining Family: Understanding the Different Forms of Family Structures

CHAPTER 2
Communication and Conflict Resolution: Building Stronger Family Relationships

CHAPTER 3
Navigating Change: Coping with Transitions and Adapting to New Norms

CHAPTER 4
Resilience and Support: Overcoming Adversity and Staying Connected

CHAPTER 5
Parenting and Child Development: Building a Strong Foundation for the Future

CHAPTER 6

Cultivating Gratitude and Appreciation: Nurturing Positive Emotions within the Family

INTRODUCTION

Families are the foundation of our lives, providing us with love, support, and a sense of belonging. But despite their importance, families can also face numerous challenges that test their bonds and relationships. Whether it's a new change or conflict, families need the right tools and strategies to strengthen their relationships and build a foundation that will last a lifetime.

This is where "Families are Forever: Strengthening Bonds in Times of Challenge" comes in. This comprehensive guide provides families with valuable insights and practical advice to help them navigate the many challenges that arise in family relationships. Through a combination of research and real-world examples, this book offers a roadmap for families to build stronger bonds and relationships that will withstand the test of time.

The book is divided into six chapters, each of which explores a different aspect of family relationships. From defining family structures and communication, to navigating change and resilience, parenting and child development, and cultivating gratitude and appreciation, this book covers all the key components of family relationships.

One of the key themes throughout the book is the importance of communication and conflict resolution. Effective communication and conflict resolution are critical to building strong relationships, and this book provides families with the tools they need to navigate conflicts and build strong bonds.

The book also explores the role of resilience and support in family relationships. Whether families are facing new challenges or simply looking to improve their relationships, resilience and support are essential components of family life. By learning how to overcome adversity and stay connected, families can build stronger and more resilient relationships.

Another important theme of the book is the role of parents and child development. The book provides guidance and advice for parents on how to help their children grow and develop into well-rounded individuals, and how to build a strong foundation for their children's future.

Finally, the book concludes with a focus on gratitude and appreciation, highlighting the many benefits of these positive emotions for families. By cultivating gratitude and appreciation, families can create a positive and supportive environment that promotes happiness and well-being for everyone.

In summary, "Families are Forever: Strengthening Bonds in Times of Challenge" is an essential guide for families looking to build stronger relationships and create a foundation that will last a lifetime. Whether you're facing new challenges or simply looking to improve your family relationships, this book provides the insights and advice you need to succeed.

Chapter 1

Defining Family: Understanding the Different Forms of Family Structures

The traditional image of a family is one with a married couple and their children, living under one roof. However, families come in many shapes and sizes and can take on a wide range of forms. Understanding the different forms of family structures is essential for promoting healthy family relationships and supporting the needs of all family members.

The first type of family structure is the traditional nuclear family, which consists of a married couple and their children. This is the most common form of family in Western societies and is often viewed as the norm. This type of family structure is characterized by a clear hierarchy, with the parents as the head of the household and the children as dependents.

Another common family structure is the single-parent family. This can occur as a result of divorce, separation, or death of a spouse, or due to the fact that the child was born out of wedlock. Single-parent families are often headed by a mother, and can face unique challenges, including financial strain and difficulty balancing the responsibilities of raising a child with work and other commitments.

Blended families are becoming increasingly common and are defined as families that are made up of individuals from two or more previously established families. This type of family structure can be challenging as family members navigate relationships with step-siblings and step-parents. However, blended families can also offer opportunities for family members to form new relationships and support systems.

Grandparents raising grandchildren is another form of family structure that is becoming increasingly common. This can occur as a result of the parents being unable to care for their children due to drug or alcohol abuse, death, or incarceration. Grandparents who take on the role of caregiver face unique challenges, including financial strain, managing the responsibilities of caring for a child, and navigating the complexities of the child welfare system.

Foster and adopted families are also a form of family structure. Foster families provide temporary care for children who have been removed from their homes due to abuse or neglect. Adopted families provide permanent care for children who cannot be reunited with their birth families. Both foster and adopted families face unique challenges, including navigating complex family dynamics and building relationships with birth families.

Intergenerational families are families that include multiple generations living together under one roof. This type of family structure can be beneficial for both young and old family members, as it provides opportunities for intergenerational relationships and support.

Finally, extended families are families that include aunts, uncles, cousins, and other relatives who are not part of the immediate family. This type of family structure can provide a strong support network, especially during times of need.

In conclusion, families come in many shapes and sizes, and it's essential to understand the different forms of family structures. This includes the traditional nuclear family, single-parent family, blended family, grandparents raising grandchildren, foster and adopted families, intergenerational families, and extended families. Understanding the unique challenges and opportunities that each family structure presents can help families to better support each other and build strong and healthy relationships.

Chapter 2

Communication and Conflict Resolution: Building Stronger Family Relationships

Communication is essential for building and maintaining strong family relationships. When family members can effectively communicate with each other, it can help to build trust, resolve conflicts, and foster a deeper understanding of each other's needs and perspectives. However, when communication breaks down, it can lead to misunderstandings, frustration, and hurt feelings.

The first step in building effective communication skills is to be an active listener. This means giving your full attention to the person speaking and trying to understand their point of view. It's also important to avoid interrupting, making assumptions, or being judgmental. By being an active listener, you show the other person that you respect and value their opinions, which can help to build trust and foster open and honest communication.

Another important aspect of communication is to express your feelings and opinions clearly and respectfully. This means avoiding aggressive or passive-aggressive behaviors and using "I" statements instead of blaming the other person. For example, instead of saying "you always do this," you could say "I feel frustrated when this happens."

Conflict resolution is another essential aspect of building strong family relationships. Conflicts are inevitable in any relationship, and when they're not effectively managed, they can lead to hurt feelings and damaged relationships. The key to effective conflict resolution is to focus on finding a solution that works for everyone involved, rather than trying to win or be right.

One effective method for resolving conflicts is to use "win-win" negotiation. This means looking for solutions that benefit everyone involved and taking the time to understand each other's needs and perspectives. It's important to avoid becoming defensive or attacking the other person and to work together to find a solution that meets everyone's needs.

Another effective method for resolving conflicts is to practice active listening and empathy. This means trying to understand the other person's perspective and feelings, and avoiding making assumptions or being judgmental. When family members can understand each other's needs and perspectives, it becomes easier to find a solution that works for everyone involved.

It's also important to establish clear boundaries and guidelines for communication and conflict resolution within your family. This can include setting ground rules for how conflicts will be resolved, such as avoiding aggressive or passive-aggressive behaviors, and seeking the help of a neutral third party if needed. Having clear guidelines can help family members to feel safe and supported, and to build stronger relationships.

Communication and conflict resolution are essential for building strong family relationships. By focusing on active listening, clear and respectful expression of feelings, and effective conflict resolution strategies, families can build trust, foster open and honest communication, and strengthen their relationships with each other. Establishing clear guidelines for communication and conflict resolution can also help families to feel safe and supported, and to build stronger relationships.

Chapter 3

Navigating Change: Coping with Transitions and Adapting to New Norms

Change is an inevitable part of life, and families are no exception. Whether it's a change in living arrangements, family dynamics, or personal circumstances, navigating change can be a challenge for everyone involved. The key to successfully coping with transitions and adapting to new norms is to have a strong support system, a positive attitude, and effective coping strategies.

The first step in navigating change is to acknowledge and accept it. This means recognizing that change is inevitable and that it can bring both positive and negative consequences. By accepting change, you can start to focus on finding ways to cope with it and make the most of the opportunities it presents.

It's also important to have a strong support system in place. This can include family, friends, support groups, or professional counseling. Having a support system can help you to feel less isolated and provide you with a source of comfort and guidance during times of transition.

In addition to having a support system, having a positive attitude can also be an important factor in navigating change. This means focusing on the opportunities and benefits of change, rather than the challenges and obstacles. A positive attitude can help you to remain optimistic and motivated, and to better cope with stress and uncertainty.

Effective coping strategies are another important aspect of navigating change. These can include healthy self-care practices, such as exercise, healthy eating, and getting enough sleep, as well as practicing stress-reducing activities such as mindfulness, yoga, or meditation. It's also important to seek out professional help if needed, such as counseling or therapy, to help you cope with the emotional challenges of change.

It's also important to stay connected with loved ones during times of change. This means reaching out to family and friends, attending community events and activities, and staying involved in organizations and activities that you care about. Staying connected with loved ones can help you to feel less isolated and provide you with a source of support and comfort during times of transition.

Navigating change can be a challenging experience, but with the right support, attitude, and coping strategies, it's possible to successfully cope with transitions and adapt to new norms. By having a strong support system, a positive attitude, and effective coping strategies, you can build resilience, maintain your well-being, and grow stronger as a family.

Chapter 4

Resilience and Support: Overcoming Adversity and Staying Connected

Families face a wide range of challenges and obstacles throughout their lives, including financial difficulties, health problems, relationship issues, and more. In order to overcome these challenges and build a strong, resilient family bond, it's important to have a supportive network in place and to develop strategies for resilience.

One of the key components of resilience is having a supportive network. This can include family members, friends, or community organizations. Having a supportive network can help families to feel less isolated and provide a source of comfort and support during difficult times. In addition, reaching out to others for help and support can build stronger relationships and foster a sense of community.

Another important factor in building resilience is having a positive attitude. This means focusing on the opportunities and benefits of difficult situations, rather than the challenges and obstacles. A positive attitude can help families to remain optimistic and motivated, and to better cope with stress and uncertainty.

Effective coping strategies are also critical to building resilience. This can include engaging in healthy self-care practices, such as exercise, healthy eating, and getting enough sleep, as well as practicing stress-reducing activities such as mindfulness, yoga, or meditation. It's also important to seek out professional help if needed, such as counseling or therapy, to help families cope with the emotional challenges of adversity.

In addition to having a supportive network and a positive attitude, families can also build resilience by staying connected with loved ones. This means reaching out to family and friends, attending community events and activities, and staying involved in organizations and activities that are meaningful to you. Staying connected with loved ones can help families to feel less isolated and provide a source of support and comfort during difficult times.

Finally, families can build resilience by developing a sense of purpose and meaning. This can include setting goals, working towards a common purpose, and finding ways to contribute to their community. By having a sense of purpose and meaning, families can stay focused and motivated, even in the face of adversity.

Overcoming adversity and building a strong, resilient family bond requires a supportive network, a positive attitude, effective coping strategies, staying connected with loved ones, and a sense of purpose and meaning. By focusing on these key components, families can build resilience, maintain their well-being, and grow stronger as a family, even in the face of challenging circumstances.

Chapter 5

Parenting and Child Development: Building a Strong Foundation for the Future

Parenting is one of the most important and rewarding roles that a person can take on. It's a journey full of challenges, but also full of joys and successes. In order to help children grow and develop to their full potential, it's important for parents to have a solid understanding of child development and to provide a supportive, nurturing environment.

One of the key components of good parenting is being attuned to a child's needs. This means paying attention to their physical, emotional, and cognitive development, and providing the necessary support and resources to help them grow and develop. Parents can do this by engaging in activities that stimulate the child's mind, such as reading, playing educational games, and providing opportunities for creative play.

Another important aspect of parenting is providing a safe and nurturing environment. This means creating a stable home environment, free from physical and emotional abuse, and providing a supportive and positive atmosphere. A safe and nurturing environment can help children feel secure and confident, and can provide a foundation for healthy development.

In addition to being attuned to a child's needs and providing a safe and nurturing environment, it's also important for parents to be involved in their child's life. This can include participating in school activities, helping with homework, and spending quality time together. By being involved in their child's life, parents can build stronger relationships with their children and provide a foundation for healthy development.

Another key component of good parenting is setting clear boundaries and expectations. This means establishing rules and guidelines for behavior, and consistently enforcing consequences for misbehavior. By setting clear boundaries and expectations, parents can help children understand what is expected of them and promote positive behavior.

Finally, good parenting involves promoting independence and self-esteem. This means encouraging children to take on new responsibilities, such as chores or hobbies, and allowing them to make their own decisions. It also means complimenting and recognizing their achievements and helping them build a positive self-image.
Parenting is a critical role that requires a solid understanding of child development, a safe and nurturing environment, involvement in the child's life, clear boundaries and expectations, and promoting independence and self-esteem. By focusing on these key components, parents can provide a strong foundation for their children's future and help them grow and develop to their full potential.

Chapter 6

Cultivating Gratitude and Appreciation: Nurturing Positive Emotions within the Family

Gratitude and appreciation are two of the most important emotions that families can cultivate. By focusing on these positive emotions, families can create a supportive and harmonious environment that fosters growth and development. In this chapter, we will explore the benefits of gratitude and appreciation and the ways in which families can cultivate these emotions.

Gratitude has been shown to have numerous benefits for mental and emotional well-being. For example, people who practice gratitude regularly experience greater happiness, lower levels of stress and anxiety, and improved relationships. These benefits are especially important for families, as gratitude can help create a positive environment that promotes happiness and well-being for everyone.

One way families can cultivate gratitude is by making it a regular part of their routine. For example, families can start the day by sharing something they are grateful for, or they can end the day by discussing what they are grateful for that day. Additionally, families can write down what they are grateful for in a journal, which can be a powerful tool for promoting gratitude.

Appreciation is another important emotion that families can cultivate. By showing appreciation and recognition for each other's strengths and contributions, families can build stronger relationships and improve overall well-being. For example, parents can acknowledge their child's achievements and help them feel proud of their accomplishments. Children, in turn, can show appreciation for their parents by expressing gratitude for their hard work and dedication.

Another way families can cultivate appreciation is by making it a habit to express gratitude and recognition regularly. For example, families can write notes of appreciation or make a special effort to show appreciation for each other's hard work and achievements. This can help create a positive and supportive environment that promotes happiness and well-being for everyone.

Finally, families can cultivate gratitude and appreciation by making it a priority to engage in activities that promote these positive emotions. For example, families can participate in volunteer work, spend time in nature, or engage in other activities that help them feel connected and appreciative of their lives.

In conclusion, cultivating gratitude and appreciation is essential for creating a positive and supportive family environment. By focusing on these positive emotions, families can improve their relationships, increase their overall well-being, and help each member of the family grow and develop to their full potential. By making gratitude and appreciation a priority, families can build strong bonds that will last a lifetime.

www.ingramcontent.com/pod-product-compliance
Lightning Source LLC
LaVergne TN
LVHW021322160826
845679LV00001B/449
9798375653822